ageless

remarkable st. louisans

ageless

remarkable st. louisans

A St. Andrew's Resources for Seniors book

Written by Mary Kimbrough

Edited by Jane Hamilton, St. Andrew's Resources for Seniors

Photography by Nancy Bridges

Book design by Werremeyer|Floresca, St. Louis

St. Andrew's Resources for Seniors is a trademark of St. Andrew's

ISBN 0-9745994-0-9

Printed in the United States of America

First Edition

Published by Pinnacle Press

St. Louis, Missouri

acknowledgements

Our deep appreciation goes to all who have made this project a success and who have contributed their support and talents to make *Ageless – Remarkable St. Louisans* an inspiration for all of us when we think of growing older.

Our sincere appreciation and gratitude go to the fifty remarkable individuals who shared their stories with us. Without them, our dream would not have become a reality.

We thank our St. Andrew's Resources for Seniors Board of Directors who created the way to put the faces to their Vision. We give tremendous appreciation to our corporate and individual sponsors who understood the purpose and provided the financial support.

Our outstanding creative team made *Ageless – Remarkable St. Louisans* a work of art. We applaud and acknowledge: Mary Kimbrough who captured the stories of these fifty fantastic St. Louisans; Nancy Bridges whose creative photography captured their spirit; Werremeyer/Floresca whose design and publication expertise made *Ageless* a delight to view; and Jane Hamilton, our editor, who added the polish to make our book shine.

We are indebted to Virginia Trent for lending her expertise and organizational skills and to Rosemary Wick and STARS Friends for providing energetic support and valuable insight. Our selection committee members, who worked countless hours to select only fifty from hundreds of outstanding individuals, are recognized for their dedication and commitment. A special thank you to Mary Alice Ryan, Jeanne Reany, and Ann Bannes whose time, effort and oversight brought everything together.

Thanks also to the Hauser Group who helped to make the community aware of the wonderful accomplishments and vitality of these St. Louisans.

Special thanks to Anna and Whitney Harris, honorary co-chairs of our celebratory event to debut *Ageless – Remarkable St. Louisans*, and to Jim Smith and the Chase Park Plaza Hotel for their participation in hosting our Gala.

And finally, special appreciation to the entire St. Andrew's staff who work tirelessly to ensure our community continues to be responsive to the needs and wants of our seniors. It is through their dedication that St. Andrew's moves closer to a society where all older adults are respected, productive, secure and fulfilled.

foreword

**"Suppose you got up in the morning
and didn't have anything to do."**

Sr. Bernard Marie Boland, age 100

The St. Andrew's Resources for Seniors Board of Directors has a wonderful Vision. They want to help create a society where all older adults are respected, productive, secure and fulfilled. It is a particularly important Vision as the 21st Century produces a tidal wave of more than 70 million Baby Boomers moving toward retirement.

It is with our Vision and the nation's ever-growing senior population in mind that St. Andrew's has created *Ageless – Remarkable St. Louisans*. This photo / essay book celebrates fifty of St. Louis' most dynamic citizens, who just happen to be 70+. They are famous and not-so-famous; they are business people and homemakers, philanthropists and volunteers, clergy and lay people, your neighbors and friends. They are our "fabulous fifty" and representative of the respect, productivity, security and fulfillment that is possible in the "post-retirement" years. These are people who laugh at the word "retirement" and certainly never plan to retire from life. They seldom have to ask themselves: "What if I get up in the morning and have nothing to do?"

Society needs to
celebrate this new
generation of seniors.
Those who continue
to give of themselves.
Who want to and
do make a difference
as they touch all
our lives.

This high energy, fast moving group gives the world a new image of passing the 70-year mark. They represent the future of aging and are an inspiration to us all.

Society needs to celebrate this new generation of seniors. Those who continue to give of themselves. Who want to and who do make a difference as they touch all our lives.

In these pages you will hear their voices, feel their spirit. You will learn what makes them get up in the morning. They will inspire you to dream of what a joy growing older can be. You will hear with your heart how they continue to contribute to the betterment of our entire community and how blessed we are that they are here. Now let us introduce you to the spirit of fifty fabulous people who are truly…

Ageless –
Remarkable St. Louisans.

Mary Alice Ryan
President and CEO

table of contents

Blooming at

Sister Bernard Marie Boland

One Hundred

She grew up on a farm, loving nature with its trees and flowers. Today, having celebrated her 100th birthday and 80 years as a Franciscan Sister of Mary, Sister Bernard Marie Boland has added to her life a new and lovely hobby: creating greeting cards decorated with pressed blossoms, often gathered by her own hands.

It was after she had retired at age 90 from hospital service — in sick rooms and operating rooms — that she learned about flower pressing from another Sister. The hobby fills out her day and fulfills her love of nature.

"Suppose you got up in the morning and didn't have anything to do?" she asked. "Wouldn't your life be empty?" She attends Mass and provides companionship to other Sisters. "I eat three meals a day and we have evening prayer," she said. "But there is still a lot left in the day. I don't care how tired I am. I can work at my cards. And then, of course, I pick the flowers. I have dogwood now, pansies and tulips."

The blooms are carefully wrapped in tissue paper and gently pressed in telephone books placed under her mattress or weighted down by bricks. Sister has created and sold — at a minimal price — thousands of cards. Her customers are friends and acquaintances and people who have received her cards from others. She gives the proceeds to charity — all toll now thousands of dollars — to help the poor, abused women, disadvantaged single mothers and their children, and other worthy causes.

"I find it wonderful at 100 years old," Sister Bernard said, "to be able to share God's blessings."

> "Now that I am 100 years old, I qualify for the old age group. We know why we are living and what we are living for. We have learned the true value of things."

With a gentle hand and a caring nature, Sister Bernard Marie Boland creates lovely pressed flower greeting cards that delight others and provide funds for charity. She has celebrated her 100th birthday and her Pearl Anniversary – 80 years – as a Franciscan Sister of Mary and sees no earthly reason to retire from sharing with others.

"If I had to pick my own epitaph it would be: 'He was fair.' Hopefully, 'fair' as in 'just,' not as in 'mediocre.'"

Taking Us Out

Robert Broeg

to the Ball Game

B ob Broeg has been called a Missouri sports legend, but his celebrity as a sportswriter, researcher and best-selling author goes far beyond his native state.

Wherever he goes, he is surrounded by fans clambering for inside information on their favorite sports personalities. The author of 20 books on baseball, Broeg is always happy to oblige with inside-the-dugout stories of the boys of summer, particularly the St. Louis Cardinals. Joe Garagiola probably describes him best: "Broeg's favorite scenario is walking down the street with Stan Musial and Dan Devine talking about Frankie Frisch."

Broeg's love of sports and encyclopedic knowledge of baseball produced an illustrious career that is still flourishing. He was sports editor for the *St. Louis Post-Dispatch* for 19 years and assistant to the publisher for eight. He is a 25-year member of the National Baseball Hall of Fame Board of Directors and an inductee into the renowned Cooperstown museum's sportswriters' wing, as well as numerous other sports halls of fame. Broeg has also served as president of the National Baseball Writers Association, and heads the St. Louis chapter of the Society of American Baseball Research. His book, *St. Louis Cardinals Encyclopedia*, co-authored with Jerry Vickery, is considered a sports classic.

Now, at the age of 85, Broeg sometimes contemplates the "eternal" aspects of baseball. "If every man has his idea of heaven" he says, "mine would be a ball game every day in the hereafter with the best players playing in their prime."

And Bob Broeg writing up the game.

Bob Broeg is an institution. Renowned as a sports writer and best-selling author, his name is synonymous with baseball and all its colorful history. His admirers say he knows more about the game than any other living human being. He says he probably loves it more than anyone else does. Both statements are accurate enough to post on the scoreboard at Busch Stadium.

Endless

Marty Bronson

Curtain Calls

For Marty Bronson, his more than 40 years in show business are "a joy, not just work."

The versatile performer, a respected veteran of both local and national television, radio, nightclubs, commercials and films, wouldn't even think of retirement. "My career," he said, "is a lot of fun. I plan to continue doing what I do."

What Bronson does is entertain. He is a singer, writer, actor, announcer, emcee, talk show host and interviewer. His personal playbill covers the full spectrum of entertainment and communications, including eight years on KSDK-TV, Channel 5; as a radio personality/disc jockey for KSD-AM; and anchor/host of pre-game shows for three World Series. Over the years, his rich singing and speaking voice has been heard on the concert stage, in musical theater and with big bands, as well as in commercials and narration voiceovers. He is also a producer – the *Sammy Davis Jr. Variety Club Telethon* in St. Louis – and an entertainment entrepreneur – owner/operator of some of city's most unique entertainment venues, including Marty's Make-Believe Ballroom at the Chase Park Plaza.

It might seem that after such a long and varied career, Bronson would want to "bring down the curtain," retire and relax. But he will have none of that. He enjoys what he does too much; he enjoys the fact that others enjoy him. "It's important to have that affirmation, to be respected and appreciated," Bronson said. "No matter what your age."

"Seniors are so valuable; they have so much experience and knowledge to share."

In the world of entertainment, Marty Bronson has done it all. He is a versatile and experienced singer, actor, emcee, interviewer, talk show host, narrator, writer, and producer for whom retirement is not an "entertaining" alternative.

A Special

Ruby Brooks

Insight

"Wisdom is our greatest gift."

When Ruby Brooks lost her eyesight to glaucoma she did not lose her desire to educate and enlighten, her caring attitude or her independent spirit. "I won't quit," she said. "I'm a people person and there are many things I want to share with others. No, you won't find me giving up."

Mrs. Brooks, 80, is a member and past president of the St. Louis Association of Colored Women, formed in 1904 to promote freedom of speech for African American women. Perhaps most important, she is an historian for the group, providing members and others insight into the history of black women and the African American experience. Mrs. Brooks knows the details of slavery, of emancipation, of the civil rights movement, and of being a minority. "These are things that are important to share with people," she said. "Not with anger or resentment, but so they will understand."

Both young and old benefit from her expertise and caring attitude. "My desire has always been to help young people," Mrs. Brooks said, "although I like to work with older people too, because of the wisdom and experience they have."

She often visits with groups of teenagers, sharing her wisdom and insight and encouraging them to strive for goals, particularly a good education. She is an inspiration to older people, helping them to better understand black history and urging them to remain active and involved.

Mrs. Brooks lives independently and regularly attends an American Red Cross adult care and enrichment program, where she is an active participant.

"God has more for me to do that just sit around," she said. "I will never give in or give up just because I'm older and have lost my sight. I have learned too much and love other people too much to do that."

Ruby Brooks, 80, may have lost her eyesight, but she has not lost her vibrant spirit or great wisdom. An expert in black history, she shares her insight with young and old alike, fostering a new understanding and expanding awareness.

A 'Dream Job'

Sister Betty Brucker

Serving Others

An admirer says of Sister Betty Brucker: "After a career that took her to the top in high-tech health care, Sister Betty switched to serving those society has left behind."

After 17 years as president of St. Mary's Health Center in St. Louis, Sister Betty elected to skip retirement and accept an invitation from Catholic Charities to launch Catholic Community Services and serve as its executive director. She oversees 11 outreach centers that provide health care and social services to 25,000 people a year. Sister Betty refers to it as her "dream job."

A 61-year member of the Franciscan Sisters of Mary, "I love people," she said. "Even as a little girl I wanted to be a Sister. Our specialty is health care."

Her expertise in health care stood her in good stead in directing and expanding the outreach centers. "At the time I took this post, there were eight centers in Catholic Charities and I was asked to add a health component to them," Sister Betty said. Long acquainted with local hospital administrators, it was easy for her to enlist their help. Three outreach centers have been added and all 11 have been "adopted" by hospitals.

The centers serve the disadvantaged through youth programs that help to keep youngsters in school and off the streets, as well as asthma control, lead screening and alcohol recovery programs among many others.

Even though her dream job sometimes requires 12-hour days, Sister Betty is undaunted. "I'm an active person and I like people," she said. "And, I have always been interested in helping the poor. That is why I remain involved."

"There is so much that older people have to offer. Seniors have many gifts that they can pass on to younger people."

Born in St. Charles, Sister Betty Brucker grew up wanting to serve others. With bachelor's and master's degrees in nursing and hospital administration, she served as a medical supervisor, director of nursing, and as president of St. Mary's Health Center for 17 years. Now, electing to forego retirement, Sister Betty continues to serve, as executive director of Catholic Charities' Catholic Community Services.

Most Important –

Helen Burns

a Friend

As a child growing up on a Mississippi farm, Helen Burns often saw her parents give milk or vegetables to those in need, and she inherited their selfless concern for others. Today, a resident of Mercy Seat Apartments in the Central West End, Mrs. Burns is something of a lay social worker and unofficial volunteer for those around her who need assistance. Most important – she is a friend.

With her heart, her patience, her religious faith and her skills, Mrs. Burns meets the special needs of her neighbors at Mercy Seat Apartments and of others in the community. She prepares food for people on weekends when they do not receive Meals on Wheels, and shops for others who cannot drive or easily leave their homes. Nursing home patients who have no family around look forward to her regular visits. She also visits neighbors who are ill and is diligent in reminding them to take their medications. A retired beautician, she styles friends' hair just to boost their morale.

The professional social worker at Mercy Seat Apartments is one of Mrs. Burns' greatest admirers: "Very often, Helen is the person I turn to and ask, 'Could you help this person with this situation?' She has never told me no. Sometimes, this means going to the person's apartment at least twice a day, but she never fails. Helen also helps frail, older neighbors with things like laundry or housekeeping. She drives other seniors to the store and to doctor's appointments. She truly cares, is concerned about others and volunteers unselfishly."

At the age of 80, Mrs. Burns is sometimes weary, but doesn't let the beneficiaries of her personal charity know it. "I don't say to God, 'I have done my duty and I'm tired. I quit.' No, I say, 'God, give me strength.'"

"I have learned over the years that we're not necessarily expected to do all these great things. Do the little things that you can do for other people. That's what is important."

Helen Burns volunteers all the time – not with an official organization – but with her heart. She continually gives of her time and herself to other seniors – friends and neighbors who need assistance, a helping hand or simply a kind word.

Still Going

Howard Coleman

Strong

A friend says of Howard Coleman: "His hobby is living and he does a good job of it. He is 93 years old and still going strong."

Coleman acknowledges the characterization and concedes that he is only semi-retired, not being one to "just sit around." That's not his style; so, he puts in a fair number of hours each week with Stifel Nicolaus & Company as an investment broker. "I still have customers," he said. "I've got my computer in my little home office and still handle some accounts. They don't want me to quit."

Coleman joined the company because he "wanted something productive to do," after retiring as vice president of marketing for Missouri-Portland Cement Company.

When he isn't working, much of the remainder of his semi-retirement time is spent as an active member of Rotary, volunteering at his church, and visiting his wife, Alice, who is a nursing home patient. Coleman has served as Rotary president, hasn't missed a noon luncheon since he joined in 1953, and is a Paul Harris Fellow of the Rotary Foundation, a special recognition of selected members. Among the many Rotary programs he supports are the Skyway Farm where underprivileged St. Louis-area children can enjoy a country atmosphere, and a program that provides loans to nursing school students.

He and his wife have long been members of Webster Hills Methodist Church where he has served as chair of the Board of Trustees, and as an enthusiastic participant in church and community service.

"That's what life is all about, isn't it?" he said. "We need to help each other. The older you get the more you feel that way."

"You're so busy when you're younger, you don't have much time to reflect on relationships with other people. As you get older, you realize how important those relationships are."

At 93, Howard Coleman says he is too young for retirement. An investment broker and long-time Rotary member, he continues to awe his clients and to actively participate in Rotary's community programs.

"The important thing for me now is to do something for someone else. It's my time to give back."

All the

Frank Costello

Right Moves

When Frank Costello suffered a severe heart attack several years ago, he began a new chapter of his life. The founder of Mid-Continent Van Service in St. Louis, he turned the business over to his two sons and set out "to give back; to do something for others."

Now, Costello, 73, provides the "wheels" – the means – for getting donated, refurbished wheelchairs to disadvantaged people who need them. He is a driver and ardent spokesperson for Wheels for the World, an organization dedicated to securing and distributing much-needed wheelchairs. Using his own truck and trailer, Costello covers thousands of miles picking up the donated wheelchairs and delivering them to prisons where they are restored by inmates and then shipped out to disabled people who otherwise would be unable to afford them. A Costello-provided semi-trailer serves as a wheelchair drop station in St. Louis.

A good friend who is wheelchair-bound helped Costello to understand the value and importance of the chairs and the mobility they provide. However, he says he is also dedicated to the wheelchair effort, "because I've come to understand that it is our responsibility as human beings to help one another. It's a God-given blessing that we have the ability to give back, to help people.

"Everyone has problems," he added. "But it's important not to become self-centered. We've got to focus on other people. I've never played golf. I don't fish. I don't hunt. All I've ever done is work, and now there is Wheels for the World. I enjoy it; I enjoy it."

Born in Indiana and a St. Louisan since 1970, Frank Costello has been in the moving business most of his life. At the age of 70 he decided it was time to move more than other people's furniture. Costello now transports donated, refurbished wheelchairs, making it possible for them to get to disabled people who otherwise would not have access to them.

Forever

Patricia Dick

Green

W hen friends and family expressed curiosity about what life was really like in a retirement community, Patricia Dick wrote a book to answer their questions. She and her husband, Frederick, moved into a retirement community several years ago for the convenience, comfort and companionship of it. "But people we know who don't live here, just couldn't seem to understand," Mrs. Dick said. "So, I decided to write about it." Her first published novel, *Sap and Green People*, is the result.

A language arts and literature teacher, Mrs. Dick wrote a number of magazine articles and spent three years in research before completing her novel. Based on real-life situations with a touch of fiction, it is the "inside" story of retirement community residents, their joys, challenges and lifestyle adjustments. The book emphasizes that older people are still vital and should be respected for their capabilities. Its title, *Sap and Green People*, comes from Psalm 92 in the Bible: "They will still yield fruit in old age; They shall be full of sap and very green."

Mrs. Dick ends her book with a prayer spoken by Marj, a retirement community resident.

"'Be with us all and protect us,' Marj prayed fervently. 'And when you can't protect us or spare us, sustain us. Everyone. Everywhere.

"'And,' Marj continued her prayer, '…please let Bill and me stay vital, stay green, to the ends of our lives. To the very, very ends.'"

"As we grow older, it is important to work at keeping life meaningful; to be full of sap and very green."

Always interested in writing, Patricia Dick was chosen for the University of Missouri's Missouri Writing Project, chosen as a Ragsdale Foundation participant, selected as a Woman of Achievement, and as a Distinguished Alumna of Albion College. Mrs. Dick taught language arts and literature in Lansing, Michigan, Evanston, Illinois, and locally in Florissant.

Fifty Years of Journalism Excellence

Martin Duggan

M artin Duggan, a St. Louis newspaperman for nearly a half-century, "retired" to other full-time endeavors: an acclaimed television program and community service.

Duggan is a founder and the host/producer of *Donnybrook*, an Emmy Award-winning televised discussion group that has been on KETC Channel 9 since 1987. He and his round-table cohorts provide lively debate on a multitude of topics.

At 82, Duggan brings a wealth of experience to the *Donnybrook* table. He worked at the *St. Louis Globe-Democrat* for 45 years, starting as an assistant in the features department and advancing to associate managing editor and editor of the editorial page. After leaving the newspaper in 1984, he pitched the *Donnybrook* idea to Channel 9 and the PBS television station agreed.

"And, we've been on ever since," Duggan said. He also co-hosts a weekly radio show, *Beat the Press*, that critiques the news and media.

"I'm not the type that goes around looking for things to do in a must-be-busy sense. But I like to be active, especially mentally," he said.

Duggan is active – and not just in media. He has served as president of the Press Club, Dismas House, the Backstoppers, the White House Laymen's Retreat League and the Marygrove Advisory Board; and as a board member for Mathews-Dickey Boys Club, St. Joseph's Institute for the Deaf and Salvation Army, among others.

There is a spiritual side as well. Duggan is a Eucharistic minister with St. Monica's Catholic Church. As such, one day a week he takes Communion to Catholic patients at Barnes-Jewish Hospital. "I cherish it," Duggan said. "I get to meet some very nice people and bring comfort to them."

"Seniors should be interested in what's going on around them and shouldn't be shy about being active politically. It's imperative to stay active – for your well-being and mental health."

A native St. Louisan, Martin Duggan has to his credit one of the longest active journalism careers in the metro area. His numerous professional, community service and civic activities have brought him many honors, including: the Nathan Hale Patriotism Award, Modern Patriot Award, the Cardinal John J. Carberry Pro-Life Award, and Media Person of the Year.

A Brand

Jerome Flance, MD

New Practice

How many physicians do you know who, after decades of healing people, spend their retirement years healing communities?

Meet Dr. I. Jerome (Jerry) Flance.

At 87, retired after 60 years of practicing medicine as a lung specialist, Dr. Flance is now practicing urban renewal. He heads a Washington University Medical Center Redevelopment Corporation program to revitalize a southeast Forest Park neighborhood.

The project has received a Housing and Urban Development grant as well as support and assistance from local businesses and organizations; and, on Dr. Flance's recommendation, McCormack, Baron & Associates joined the effort as the management team.

Prior to the revitalization program, the neighborhood was without a strategically located school, community center and senior citizens' programs. "Housing was in bad shape with a number of slum landlords. Over 50 percent of the population was at poverty level or below," Dr. Flance said.

Much now is changing. A refurbished school serves neighborhood youngsters. A community center and a senior citizen assisted living facility are available. There are parks and recreational activities, and an unemployment rehabilitation program and other social services are ongoing. Neighborhood residents are actively involved in the revitalization process.

Just as he encourages the neighborhood residents to be activists, Dr. Flance urges older adults like himself to be actively occupied. "Get involved in something," he said. "Do what you have talent in that can offer something in a positive way. It's very ego-building and satisfying."

"It doesn't take a rocket scientist to know that many people aren't ready to retire at 65. We still have so much to offer and the physical and mental strength to carry it out."

Born in Brooklyn,
New York, Dr. Jerry
Flance came to
Missouri to attend
Washington University
School of Medicine.
Little did he know
that after six decades
of healing St. Louisans,
he would turn his
attention to healing
the city's
neighborhoods.

"I retired...
got bored, and
returned to work
part-time; it was
the right answer
for me."

Two Times

John Fries, MD

the Artist

For Dr. Jack Fries there is the art of healing and... art.

After serving as chief of radiology for 32 years at St. Anthony's Medical Center, Dr. Fries retired, only to return to work at another hospital and to pursue a "very serious hobby" – painting.

"I didn't really care for retirement," he said. "I retired in 1988, got bored, and returned to work part-time. That was the right answer for me." Now, he reports to St. Louis University Hospital at 5.30 a.m. every Tuesday and Thursday. There he confers with the doctors who worked the night before and reviews the work of residents.

He made his choice of a medical career as a teenager. "My family had many doctors, and they did influence my decision to become a physician," Dr. Fries said. "But you have to make your own choices in life. It has to come from within."

His other vocation – artist – is also a choice that came from within him. "It is a serious hobby," he said. One that brings him pleasure and satisfaction. The artwork – watercolor landscapes, structures and a variety of other subjects – on the walls of his home attest to the artistic side of his life.

"I didn't have any early art training because there wasn't time when I was in medical school, and I didn't start painting until I took another doctor into my practice, giving me more free time," Dr. Fries said. He has studied with various artists and attended frequent workshops in what became two of his favorite places to paint – Rockport, Massachusetts and Monterey, California.

Retirement is not for him. There is too much to be done - as a radiologist, as an artist. He thrives on being both.

A native St. Louisan, Dr. Jack Fries is a "retired" physician who continues to practice both the healing arts and the art of painting. He earned his medical degree from Louisiana State University and did his residency at St. Louis County Hospital. His artist's "residency" was served with various artists in beautiful locations that he would one day paint.

"I'm a Type A personality; it just doesn't occur to me to switch gears and sit down. I prefer to keep moving."

A Ministry

Rev. Evlyn Fulton

'Pioneer'

Daughter of a Presbyterian minister and heir to a strong religious faith, the Rev. Evlyn Fulton naturally was attracted to a career in the ministry. "The church was the life of our family," she said. "I knew early on that I wanted to be involved." And so, she enrolled in a Presbyterian seminary – in the church's first class of women seminarians.

When she graduated in 1949, there was celebration, but no ordination. "At that time the church was not ordaining women," Rev. Fulton said. "And, it never occurred to any of us to challenge the system." It wasn't until the 1970s, when the Presbyterian Church recognized the ordination of women, that Rev. Fulton fully realized her dream.

In the meantime, she had established the basis of her ministerial career, administration. In that role, she was involved in church administrative activities, pastoral work with the clergy, and in mediation.

She is best known in St. Louis as former Executive Presbyter of the Giddings-Lovejoy Presbytery. She was, in fact, involved in the union of the two presbyteries; they had split during the Civil War. "Southeast Missouri was southern, and Elijah Parish Lovejoy was northern," Rev. Fulton said. "We were able to bring the two together in the 1970s – the Presbytery of Giddings-Lovejoy. Giddings was the evangelist and Lovejoy was a social activist."

In 2002, as a longtime volunteer chaplain and board member of Doorways, a residential facility for people with AIDS, she received the Michael Edlin Award for Leadership in Providing Service for People with HIV.

At age 80, Rev. Fulton continues to serve. The personal qualities she brings to her vocation? "Enthusiasm... commitment. I'm genuinely fond of people and I believe that I work pretty well with them. I guess I just bring who I am."

Evlyn Fulton became one of the Presbyterian church's first ordained female ministers. She served as Executive Presbyter of the Presbytery of Giddings-Lovejoy for ten years, as well as with the General Assembly office in Louisville, Kentucky; as Interim Executive Presbyter in Seattle, Washington; as Interim Pastor for Northminster Presbyterian Church in St. Louis; as an instructor at Ramses College for Women in Cairo, Egypt; and on the boards of Beirut University and the Interfaith Partnership.

A Passion

Alice Gerdine

for the Arts

When she was only 5, Alice Gerdine saw her first theatrical play. By the age of 7, she was singing solos in church programs, and at 9 was taking piano lessons. She loved it all, and that set the stage for Mrs. Gerdine, now 98, to become a musical artist, a life-long patron of the arts and an enthusiastic supporter of cultural St. Louis.

Sharing a special love of theater, she and her late husband, Leigh Gerdine, were instrumental in founding the St. Louis Grand Opera in 1970. On a hot July evening, the couple was among hundreds of people packed into a college gymnasium to see an operatic performance when members of the orchestra refused to play until they were paid.

"There was no money in the till, so the hat was passed and enough money was collected for the opera to go on," Mrs. Gerdine said. "On the way home, Leigh said, 'Alice, if the people of St. Louis want opera that badly, it's time we give them a first rate opera house.' And that started it." The Gerdines enlisted other patrons of the arts, musicians and supporters to create what is now the Opera Theatre of St. Louis. She continues to contribute to the St. Louis cultural community, serves in the Volunteer Association of the St. Louis Symphony and, among other honors, was selected as a Woman of Achievement for her contributions.

It is important, Mrs. Gerdine indicated, to be passionate about *something*, "because you have to have a reason for being," she said. "All my life, I've been interested in the arts. Other people have other passions. But no matter what they are, you have to keep on trying, keep on taking part."

"I've never considered myself a very wise person, but I think I have a very young soul."

Born in South St. Louis of German heritage, Alice Gerdine was nurtured in the arts by her mother. She began musical training in voice and piano in her childhood and often accompanied her mother to the symphony and plays. The result was a life-long passion for the arts that Alice Gerdine, at 98, continues to share with and cultivate among thousands of St. Louisans.

There's Much

Rev. William Gillespie

to Save

"What is important is to do something that makes a difference."

As a young man, he planned to be a doctor and was accepted into medical school. But then, the Rev. William Gillespie decided instead to become a minister. Now, 47 years later, he is a clergyman who saves not only souls, but also the earthly neighborhoods where they reside.

After graduating from Johnson C. Smith Seminary in North Carolina, Rev. Gillespie came to St. Louis in 1956 at the request of the Presbytery to restore Cote Brilliante Presbyterian Church on the city's near north side. Most of the original congregation were gone. The neighborhood was in decline. The church had closed its doors.

Today, with the benefit of Rev. Gillespie's tenure and leadership, Cote Brilliante is a dynamic church with a large congregation in a neighborhood that is experiencing revitalization. The transformation, he says, is attributable first to a higher power and then down-to-earth social activism. The soft-spoken minister has lead the way in demonstrations and marches to rid the neighborhood of drugs and dealers; in establishing a tutoring program for area school children, a monitoring program benefiting troubled or needy youngsters, a neighborhood food pantry; and most recently in partnering with St. Andrew's Resources for Seniors to build a HUD-funded, 38-unit apartment building on church property for low-income elderly. And, all of that only scratches the surface.

Yet, even after so many years of service, Rev. Gillespie has no plans to retire. "We have to keep going," he said. "It's not beneficial to simply mark time." What is important – for people of all ages – "is to do something that makes a difference."

Rev. William Gillespie had originally planned to be a doctor – and save lives. Instead, he became something equally important – a minister bent on saving not only souls, but also neighborhoods.

Food for
Marvin Goldford
Thought

To Marvin Goldford the best way to spend retirement is feeding hungry people, encouraging older athletes, and helping handicapped children. What would seem to be full time jobs for numerous people, 78-year-old Goldford accomplishes by volunteering with Operation Food Search, the St. Louis Senior Olympics and the Variety Club. He uses the experience and knowledge he gained in the food service industry to be a very effective volunteer.

Goldford started working in his father's East St. Louis grocery as a teenager and later sold wholesale groceries, worked for a national food company and before his retirement owned a food brokerage company.

"This community has been very good to me," he said. "I have a good life and God has been very good to me. I feel that I really need to give something back, and I enjoy it tremendously, " Goldford said.

He is chair emeritus – after serving as chair for five years – of the board of Operation Food Search, an organization battling hunger since 1981. He actively creates contacts for food donations to 300 area food pantries that feed more than 95,000 people a month in Missouri and Illinois. Using his connections in food brokerage, he secures donated fruit, snack items, gift certificates and coupons to fill the "goody bags" distributed to participants in the Senior Olympics, And, as an active member of the Variety Club, he serves on the organization's allocations committee, interviewing and evaluating the children's services organizations that request Variety Club funding.

"I have a lot of energy and I never want to *really* retire," Goldford said. "I want to keep my mind and body active; I want to keep going all the time."

Marvin Goldford was raised in East St. Louis where he learned the basics of the food service industry from his father, a grocer. Now, after years of experience in the food brokerage business, he utilizes his knowledge and expertise to help feed the hungry, provide refreshments for weary Senior Olympians, and to assist disadvantaged and disabled children.

"There are a lot of different ways to be active and to help people. You find your little niche and do what you can."

A Particular

Jamie Graham

Kind of Joy

Jamie Graham probably would not classify herself as a "party animal." She is a librarian, author, historian and mentor. But it is her parties that bring her a particular kind of joy. She gives them for friends, neighbors, and acquaintances who are suffering hard times, such as a death in the family, personal disappointments and illness.

"When I see someone who is having some bad experiences, I find an occasion to give them a party," Mrs. Graham said. "They make up the invitation list and bring however many guests they want." There is a sharing of food, fellowship and helpful support. "It makes a lot of people happy," she said. "I get my joy out of seeing them enjoy themselves."

A St. Louis resident since 1951, Mrs. Graham has degrees in history and library science. She initially went into teaching. But after a librarian friend asked her to help with a library project, she switched careers because, "it was so much fun."

Over the years, Mrs. Graham has served as a librarian for public libraries, universities, corporations, and the U.S. Army. Now in her 80s, she is particularly fond of doing historical research and devising ways to make research and reference work more efficient.

A long-time member of Cote Brilliante Presbyterian Church, Mrs. Graham has written its history as well as a handbook for church youth. She is active in church service groups and a willing mentor for young people who benefit from her experience and guidance.

"There are a lot of different ways to be active and to help people," Mrs. Graham said. "You find your little niche and do what you can."

Jamie Graham is a librarian, historian, mentor and the hostess of special parties that brighten other people's lives. In her professional career, she served as Engineering Reference librarian for McDonnell Douglas Corp., as chief of the Reference & Research Library at the U.S. Army Aviation Command, as urban bibliographer for Washington University Libraries, as chair of the Urban Affairs Division and Positive Action Committee of the Special Libraries Association, and as president of the St. Louis Chapter of the Special Libraries Association and the St. Louis Library Club.

Peg of Our

Margaret Grigg

Hearts

Many call her "Peg of Our Hearts."

She is Margaret (Peg) Grigg, a native St. Louisan who, now in her 80s, is an ardent supporter of St. Louis' cultural institutions. Among the beneficiaries of her generosity are the St. Louis Symphony Orchestra, Missouri Historical Society, The Sheldon, St. Louis Art Museum, Missouri Botanical Garden and the Eugene Field House. With the passing years and ongoing problems with her sight, Mrs. Grigg cannot be as physically active as she would like. However, she frowns on apathy and urges: "If you have an interest in something, be involved. I don't believe in sitting back and letting the grass grow."

Her involvement and generosity are "growing" many of St. Louis' cultural treasures. And, while she is reluctant to talk about herself and her charitable efforts, others are happy to do so.

Robert Archibald, president of the Missouri Historical Society, says of Peg Grigg: "She is unparalleled in giving of herself and of funding. And she has been doing that for us at M.H.S. for more than 50 years."

Richard Gaddes, Opera Theatre of St. Louis, says, "It wouldn't be St. Louis for me if she wasn't here."

When Richard Hayman is in town to conduct the Symphony orchestra, he often whips out his harmonica and dedicates "Peg of My Heart" to her. He says of the Symphony musicians: "They're so good. I just give them a downbeat and get out of their way. Peg has a lot to do with the fact that we can afford that kind of quality."

Mrs. Grigg is quick to thank people for their appreciation and slow to take the credit. "St. Louis is a wonderful city," she said. "We're so fortunate to have so many cultural treasures to enjoy."

"St. Louis is a wonderful city to be enjoyed by young and old alike."

A native St. Louisan, Margaret Grigg - Peg to all who know her- has for many years been an enthusiastic supporter of St. Louis' cultural venues. The Symphony, Historical Society, Art Museum and Botanical Garden are only a few of the institutions that have benefited from her financial and philosophical support. Exceedingly modest and exceptionally generous, she contributes greatly to the city's cultural well-being.

"With age comes wisdom, an understanding of the past and a deep appreciation for the future."

A Place

Whitney Harris

in History

Whitney Harris is one of the most distinguished and honored men not only in St. Louis, but throughout America and in Europe where he was part of the post-World War II legal staff that prosecuted major German war criminals at the Nuremberg trials.

A book he authored in 1954 on that defining experience, *Tyranny on Trial. The Evidence at Nuremberg*, was described by the *New York Times* as "the first complete historical and legal analysis of the Nuremberg trial; a book of enduring importance." A second edition was published in1995 and a third in 1999.

Harris entered the United States Navy as an Ensign in 1942. He served as a line officer through most of World War II, but toward the end was assigned for special duty with the Office of Strategic Services and placed in charge of the investigation of war crimes in the European theater. In this capacity he was responsible for the prosecution of Ernst Kaltenbrunner, the Gestapo and the SS. A delegate to the Rome Conference for the International Criminal Court, Harris represented the Committee of Former Nuremberg Prosecutors of which he was organizer and coordinator.

He has said of that era, "Nuremberg and Rome stand against the resignation of humankind to its self-debasement and self-destruction. The achievement of that great trial and historic conference in elevating justice and law over inhumanity and war give promise for a better tomorrow."

A passage from Harris' book speaks to any era: "Tyranny leads to inhumanity, and inhumanity is death. Let us resolve that tyranny shall not extend its sway, nor war become its game — placing our faith in the cause of justice, in the freedom of man, and in the mercy of God."

Whitney Harris graduated magna cum laude from the University of Washington and holds a Juris Doctor Degree from the University of California. His efforts in the prosecution of German war criminals brought him many honors, including the Legion of Merit of the United States; the Order of Merit, Officers' Class, of Germany; and the Medal of the War Crimes Commission of Poland. In 1980, he established the *Whitney R. Harris Collection on the Third Reich of Germany* at Washington University where the Whitney R. Harris Institute on Global Studies was named for him in 2002.

More Than

Jean Hobler

a Dance

"At the center of the earth there is only dance." It is one of Jean Hobler's favorite quotes from T. S. Eliot. "I have always loved to dance," she said. "It has always been an important part of my life." But in recent years, the center of Jean Hobler's world has shifted dramatically, from dance and involvement in numerous civic and service organizations to ALS – Lou Gehrig's Disease. Her son, Christopher, was diagnosed with it in 2000.

Once, an accomplished musician; a husband and father, Christopher, 37, "can no longer see, cannot walk, can talk only with effort, and has trouble even holding a glass," Mrs. Hobler said. Life expectancy for those afflicted with ALS is three to five years.

She and her husband, Wells, have started a foundation – ALS Hope – dedicated to medical research and hopefully, one day, a cure for the deadly disease which causes devastating degeneration of the nervous system. "We want to establish a center for the study of 'orphan diseases,' very rare diseases like ALS, where scientists from different fields can cross fertilize their findings and ideas," Mrs. Hobler said.

Christopher is the third family member to develop Lou Gehrig's Disease. "My father died of ALS at 81," she said, "and, one of my nephews also has it."

With the stamina of a dancer, the concern of a civic-minded volunteer, and a mother's love, Jean Hobler continues on. "My question is always: 'What can I do to help; what can I do that needs to be done?'" she said. "Someone once asked me: 'How would you want to be remembered?' I'm not exactly sure; but, I do know that I wouldn't want to be remembered as someone who sat back and did nothing."

Jean Hobler, long invloved in the arts and community service, was part of Dance St. Louis from its inception and has served many times on the board of directors. She has served on the International Council of Arts and Letters, the National Council of Arts and Science, and on the Board of Trustees at Webster University. A Hobler donation to Webster University produced two large dance studios and associated facilities.

"Smell the roses
and listen to good
music and the birds.
Share with others
and spread joy
somewhere."

Career

Thomas Hood

About-Face

I n some ways, Tom Hood did a complete "career about-face" when retirement rolled around. He retired from the corporate world and began a new calling within the religious community. The former employee manager for Xerox Corporation has served for almost 10 years now at many levels of the Presbyterian Church (USA).

Hood began his second career as professional staff for church development and redevelopment. He also served as Associate Executive Presbyter for Community Ministries and as the Presbytery's representative to the General Assembly at the national level of the denomination.

He currently chairs the National Ministries Division of the General Assembly Council with oversight for church-wide ministries ranging from higher education and social justice to urban, racial, ethnic and women's ministries. In his "home" church, Cote Brilliante Presbyterian, he is an ordained elder very much involved in community outreach.

"It's not necessarily the preaching and the singing that bring people to a church, although they enjoy that," Hood said. "It's the outreach, what the church is doing in the community. People really want to be part of that." That, he says, applies to himself and is one of the major reasons he made the leap from corporate to spiritual work.

"I felt there was something that I could give back to this denomination and to humankind in general, something that hopefully could make life better," he said. "If I have something to offer, then I want to share."

Regardless of age or career.

"The world needs all kinds of people and that's why we have all kinds of them, with different gifts. Seniors have the gifts of knowledge and experience to share."

With a professional history that includes Army veteran, bus driver, postal worker, and corporate management, Thomas Hood's retirement career is with the church. A graduate of Saint Louis University, he retired from big business in 1994 to serve in a variety of important positions with the Presbyterian Church (USA).

"People sometimes say to me, 'We came to the Fox Theatre when we were young and listened to you play the organ. Aren't you 106 by now?' And, I say 'Not at all – 107.'"

Play It

Stan Kann

Again, Stan

He began "playing" the windowsill at the age of 4 while listening to the radio and was at the organ by the time he reached 14. For Stan Kann, it was the start of an enduring, decades-long career as a musician, comedian and all-around entertainer.

Today, in his 70s, he is still one of the best-known theater organists in America and one of St. Louis' most popular performers.

For 22 years, beginning in the 1950s, Kann played the St. Louis Fox Theatre's mighty Wurlitzer pipe organ. He was, in fact, instrumental in its restoration from years of disuse and neglect. He continues to appear at the Fox, popular local restaurants, area churches, synagogues and other venues, while still finding time and energy for concert tours in the U.S. and Europe.

"I love it so much, I cannot tell you," Kann said. "It's when I'm doing something for and with people that I feel really good."

His musical ability, natural comedic talents, and somewhat unusual hobby of collecting vacuum cleaners – last count, he owned 132 of the machines – have resulted in multiple TV appearances. He was a favorite on all the major talk shows in the '70s, '80s and '90s, appearing with celebrities such as Johnny Carson dozens of times and making life-long friendships with the likes of comedienne Phyllis Diller.

"Every once in a while," Kann said, "I wish I were just beginning my career. If you feel there's something for you to do, and you're exuberant about it and have joy, you're going to do it."

Born in St. Louis' Central West End, Stan Kann displayed an early talent for music. Now, decades later, he is still considered the premier theater organist. He is an inductee of the American Theater Organ Society Hall of Fame, a recipient of the American Guild of Organists' Avis Blewitt Award, and one of St. Louis' most enduring entertainers.

A Stitch

Michael & Katharina Kegler

in Time

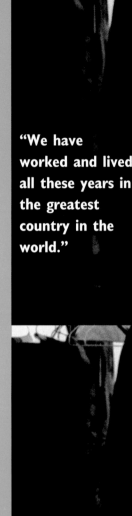

A mid the turmoil of World War II, Michael Kegler was determined to escape his native Romania for a new life and to pursue his goal: to become one of the world's finest tailors. So, he slipped away unnoticed on a train to Vienna, where he would study and work in Viennese tailor shops to learn the art of his chosen profession. His wife, Katharina, joined him. And, within a decade they journeyed to St. Louis, where relatives lived, and opened what is perhaps the most enduring and successful tailoring shop in the city.

"I wanted to make a suit so fine that a man would pay $5,000 for it, but also would smile, shake my hand and be happy about it," Michael Kegler said.

From the number and names of his St. Louis patrons, he did just that.

Michael is 88. Katharina is 80. Yet, each weekday still finds them at their shop. Katharina is Michael's only employee, his seamstress. When he designs a suit, recommends the fabric and cuts the pattern, she uses her own special skills to do the detail work. Each of their creations is unique; the product of pure tailoring.

On the wall of their shop are words the Keglers can read each day: "Every man to his business, but indeed the craft of the tailor is beyond all doubt as noble and as secret as any in the world."

They have no definite plans regarding retirement – perhaps when Michael is 90. Perhaps. They have after all, they say, been able to work long beyond the average person's working years "in the greatest country in the world" and been happy.

If no "alterations" are necessary why make them?

> "We have worked and lived all these years in the greatest country in the world."

Having fled Romania more than 50 years ago, Michael and Katharina Kegler are in their 80s and providing St. Louis premier tailoring. There are no pre-cut patterns or shortcuts; each of their creations is one-of-a-kind.

"I have compassion for people who are in need and so I do what I can."

Feeding the

Samantha Kendall

Lambs

"I am in awe of what she is able to do," says Jean Kendall in describing her mother, Samantha. "She lives what she believes: that you are never too old to take on new challenges, to help other people, and to live life to the full."

Samantha Kendall, 80 years young, appreciates her daughter's loving evaluation, but is modest about her own efforts. A deeply religious woman, Mrs. Kendall says she is simply trying to live her Christian beliefs. "Jesus said: 'You will do greater work than I do.'" she points out. "I'm not trying to do greater work. I'm just trying to feed his lambs."

Those lambs include children, young people and other seniors who have needs that Samantha Kendall busily tries to meet. Twice each week, she reads to youngsters in a Head Start program. She conducts Bible study for the residents of a home for teenaged unwed mothers. The Bessie M. Pointer Scholarship Fund, founded by Mrs. Kendall, has provided more than $400,000 in scholarships to St. Louis young people.

At her church, Mrs. Kendall teaches Sunday school classes for both children and adults, and regularly visits nursing home residents and hospital patients. She is chaplain for the Fifth District Lay Organization of the African Methodist Episcopal Church, a district that encompasses the western half of the United States. She recently returned from a missions trip to Cape Town, Africa, where a much-needed health center is being constructed.

"I do believe the Lord wants us to do for others, and so I try my best," Mrs. Kendall said. "It's a blessing, because I think I get more out of it than they do."

A native of Arkansas and a St. Louis resident for more than 50 years, Samantha Kendall is rooted firmly in her Christian beliefs – beliefs that include ministering to other people. Throughout her life, and particularly during her later years, she has made it a point to "help feed God's lambs."

Behind the

Mary Kimbrough

Headlines

S he is a master storyteller and a veteran journalist with a passion for writing that has fueled a career that spans more than 60 years. Mary Kimbrough believes, "The art and science of communication is so important. We must know what is going on in the world and we should be involved. Writing is one way to get involved."

As an author, a news reporter, feature writer, columnist and editor for several major newspapers her words have delighted and informed millions of people. Those she has interviewed include Eleanor Roosevelt and just about every major personality, politician and interesting individual in the St. Louis area.

She is the author of 15 books, including *A History of the Muny Opera*, *Movers and Shakers*, a compilation of feature stories about recipients of the *St. Louis Globe-Democrat's* Man of the Year Award, *Behind the Headlines*, a history of the *Globe-Democrat*, and *The Joy and Adventure of Growing Younger*, a candid look at aging.

Now in her 80s, Ms. Kimbrough continues to interview, research and write. She is writing the biography of a local businessman, provides articles to *Senior Circuit*, and is the writer who profiled fellow honorees on other pages of *Ageless – Remarkable St. Louisans*.

"I can't imagine ever giving up writing," she said. It is something she loves as a means of "telling important stories and keeping people informed." It is also a very effective way for her to remain involved, to continue to contribute.

"Seniors have such a wealth of experience that they can share," she said. "Everyone has something to give; they just have to be alert to the possibilities."

Mary Kimbrough's "possibilities" are awesome.

"We have to continue to exercise our minds, our bodies and our skills, or all will fade away."

A journalist for more than six decades, Mary Kimbrough was a reporter and editor for the *St. Louis Globe-Democrat* and the *St. Louis Post-Dispatch* before retiring to author books and to do freelance writing. Her ability to discover and describe has brought many honors, including being named National Headliner by and elected national president of Theta Sigma Phi (Women in Communications); being selected for the Woman of Achievement and the Woman of Worth awards; being chosen Media Person of the Year; and receiving the University of Missouri Medal for Distinguished Journalism.

"If I don't work, I don't feel I can relax."

One to

Walter Knoll

Grow On

He is the second generation of a family that has been growing flowers, cultivating plants and bringing beauty to St. Louis homes since 1885. Walter Knoll, 70, has no immediate plans to hang up the flower shears or store away the fertilizer.

He goes to work every day, even though he has passed the business along to his sons, and can be tracked down in one of the family's seven flower shops.

"If I don't work, I don't feel I can relax," Knoll said. "I like being busy, being involved."

The Knoll Flower Company, founded by Knoll's father, was one of the first commercial flower growers in the United States and became known for its American Beauty roses.

One of Knoll's earliest memories is of his father's little greenhouse on Gravois in south St. Louis near where Walter was born. He remembers tagging along after the horse-drawn wagon in which his father transported flowers and plants to market.

Knoll graduated from Southwest High School and the Washington University School of Retailing. He says, with a grin, that he was a "misfit" in the school where students were learning the ways of big business.

"I did learn how big business operates," Knoll said. "But it is also true that ours is a business with a personal touch." That personal touch and family heritage are two of the reasons Knoll remains involved – that, plus the fact, "It's fun."

Walter Knoll knows all about the art of growing things. He has been in the flower business since childhood and now, at 70, has no intention of retiring from the sweet scent of fresh cut flowers, the beauty of blooming plants and the pleasure they bring to people.

"We all have the same goals. We want to be respected, to feel that we're making a contribution, that we're needed."

A Journey

Desmond Lee

of Hope

Des Lee once described his philanthropy as "an exciting journey of hope." He said: "Our journey will never reach the final destination of 'having accomplished.' The 'doing' is everything. The 'having done' is nothing."

Lee's ongoing philanthropic journey is a boon to the community in which he has lived most of his life. The owner of Lee-Rowan Company, manufacturer of wire shelving, baskets and closet organizers, is a benefactor and civic leader.

With the belief that, "The greatest needs are to assist the under-served, particularly children, through education," Lee established the Des Lee Collaboration Vision in conjunction with the University of Missouri – St. Louis and Washington University. The program encompasses 27 endowed professorships and involves five other area colleges and universities and more than 100 member organizations. He has also been a benefactor to and served on the boards of directors of numerous civic organizations, including the YMCA, Herbert Hoover Boys and Girls Club, Ranken Technical College, St. Louis Science Center, St. Louis Symphony, St. Louis Zoo, Missouri Botanical Garden, Missouri Historical Society, and Variety Club of St. Louis.

Lee attributes his social awareness to his father and to lessons learned with his employees and troops he commanded in World War II. How would he like to be remembered? Lee says simply: "As a person who loved working with people and bringing out the best in them."

Des Lee's philanthropic efforts and civic leadership have brought him numerous awards. *WORTH Magazine* listed him among the 100 most generous Americans. A graduate of the Washington University School of Business, he is a recipient of the university's Distinguished Alumni Award. He received an honorary degree, Doctorate of Humane Letters, from the University of Missouri-St. Louis and was named St. Louis Man of the Year among many other honors.

The Sound

Harriett Lee

of Music

In Harriett Lee's north side home, a piano is the dominant piece of furniture and music often fills the air. Music has always been a major part of her life. Her mother was a choir director and her father, who was president of Florida A & M College, played several musical instruments. Harriett, who began taking piano lessons at the age of 3, graduated from Fisk University with a degree in music.

Today, she is a nationally known musician, a church organist, pianist and choir director who was once invited by First Lady Eleanor Roosevelt to bring a choir to the White House to perform for the Queen of England. Accompanist to many great artists, such as Roland Hayes, Lilly Evanti and Clarence Cameron Chite, Mrs. Lee has also played with the St. Louis Symphony Orchestra and many times on radio. But throughout her career, she has nourished her talent with her faith.

"Music is my field and I was brought up in the church," she said. "I have always remembered that my grandfather, a Congregationalist minister in North Carolina, used to say that if there were no minister in the church, the choir could give the sermon. And so, when I direct a church choir, I try to choose numbers that would be as a sermon." She has served as organist and choir director at Cote Brilliante Presbyterian Church in St. Louis for 47 years.

For Mrs. Lee, there are no plans to retire from her music and the pleasure of sharing it with others. Her intent, she says, is that her home, her church, and her life will always be filled with the sound of music.

"There is no greater gift we can give as seniors than ourselves and what we have learned over the years."

Born into a musical family, Harriett Lee began taking piano lessons at the age of 3. The sound of music has been with her ever since. She is an award winning music teacher, pianist, organist, accompanist, recitalist and choir director who has performed with great artists before heads of state. And perhaps most important to her — at her church for nearly half a century.

Super

John Londoff

Salesman

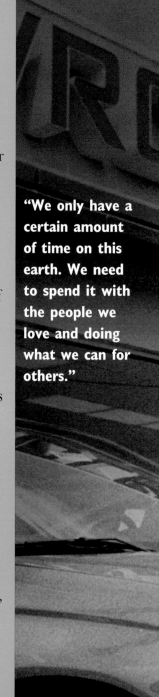

Johnny Londoff could, by some newspaper accounts, "...sell a case of beer to August Busch III., a sorehead bear with a toothache to the St. Louis Zoo; trade a secondhand Edsel to Henry Ford for a new Lincoln Continental and give the change to a worthy cause."

Londoff, 78, a celebrity-caliber Chevrolet dealer for many years and a super salesman for good causes, is one of the most active and honored civic leaders in the St. Louis area.

As longtime chair of the annual *Sammy Davis Jr. Variety Club Telethon*, Londoff set fundraising records – more than $42 million over the years for disabled and disadvantaged St. Louis children – by persuading Davis and other major stars to lend their talents to the cause.

He and his wife, Sylvia, were instrumental in raising more than $1million for a state-of-the-art center at St. Louis Children's Hospital that serves youngsters with neurological and orthopedic illnesses and injuries.

"You know, we all have only a certain amount of time on this earth," Londoff said. "And it seems to me we need to spend it developing relationships with the people we love and doing what we can to help others."

Londoff's most important relationships are with his wife and their four children. They are all his inspiration, but none more than Jackie, the Londoffs' special child, born 42 years ago with Downs Syndrome. "Jackie has taught me so much and brought us such great joy," Londoff said.

When Londoff attempted to respond to a public tribute from Children's Hospital and was too overcome with emotion to speak, Jackie took his note cards, walked to the podium, and gave his speech for him.

"That's Jackie," he said. "There wasn't a dry eye in the house."

"We only have a certain amount of time on this earth. We need to spend it with the people we love and doing what we can for others."

Johnny Londoff, a super salesman of cars and for good causes, has raised millions of dollars for local charities. A college scholarship program he established has awarded more than 400 scholarships. His awards are numerous and include: St. Louis Children's Hospital Heart of Gold Award, *Time Magazine's* Quality Dealer Award for which community involvement is a determining factor, the *St. Louis Globe-Democrat* Humanities Award, St. Louis Variety Club Man of the Year and Variety International's Presidential Citation.

How Sweet

Helen Lubeley

It Is

With the warm, fragrant aroma of fresh baked goods drifting around her, Helen Lubeley feels "wonderful." What she does not feel is 90 years old. "Yes, I'm 90," Mrs. Lubeley said. "But I don't think time has slowed me up."

Time doesn't stand a chance where Helen Lubeley is concerned. A 65-year veteran of the bakery business, she still arrives at 6:30 a.m. each day at the family-owned bakery / deli to help bake delicious goodies, wait on customers, shop for groceries and even, at times, wash dishes and clean up the shop.

"I think if you just sit at home, it makes you old," Mrs. Lubeley said. "You have to go on keeping busy, meeting people and making a difference."

It was her late husband, Edward, who introduced her to the bakery business. "I was a store girl in Kirkwood and Edward was a baker," Mrs. Lubeley said. "He was going to be laid off, so he said, 'That's it. We're going to go into business.' We opened our first bakery in 1937 on Kingshighway." With an ever growing number of customers, the couple moved to larger quarters in Maplewood, then Yorkshire Village, and finally the current location on Watson Road.

Perhaps Mrs. Lubeley has made one concession to time. She has turned the bakery's ownership over to her son and daughter. "So, I'm their employee," she said with a grin. "I'm the cheapest one they've got."

Perhaps the "cheapest," but certainly not the least valued.

"I think if you just sit at home, it makes you old."

Helen Lubeley, 90, arrives early every morning at the family bakery, just as she has done for 65 years. She has probably touched the short, sweet lives of millions of dough-nuts in that time, but has no intention of hanging up her apron.

"Someday I want to be able to look back and think that I have made a difference."

A Character–Building

Sanford and Priscilla McDonnell

Experience

During his career as chair of McDonnell Douglas, Sanford (Sandy) McDonnell concentrated on wings and sky. But with retirement, he worried more about what was happening on earth – a seemingly drastic decline in old-fashioned ethics and integrity.

"We have too many 12-year-olds pushing drugs, 14-year-olds having babies, 16-year-olds killing each other," McDonnell said. "And young people are admitting, in epidemic levels, to lying, cheating and stealing. I believe that building good character is crucial to correcting those problems and is the basis of all of our freedoms."

That belief inspired McDonnell and his wife, Priscilla, to create CHARACTER*plus*, a school-based character education program designed to help young people build personal character and integrity.

The basis of CHARACTER*plus* came out of McDonnell's long involvement in Boy Scouts of America. He is former national president of the organization. "After years of telling young people to live up to the Scout oath and law, I asked myself what kind of character training youngsters were getting in school and realized there was no formal training," McDonnell said. "So, we started CHARACTER*plus* in seven St. Louis County school districts." Today, the program is in 440 schools in the St. Louis region and involves more than 250,000 students. Another 150,000 participate in outstate Missouri. There is also a national organization, the Character Education Partnership, headquartered in Washington, D.C. McDonnell is chair of its board of directors.

"I feel that I couldn't have chosen a better way to serve my country in retirement," McDonnell said, "than by helping young people become honest, responsible, respectful, caring, hard-working citizens with high moral courage."

For Sanford and Priscilla McDonnell it's a matter of character. Concerned about a perceived decline in integrity and ethics among young people, the McDonnells created CHARACTER*plus*, a school-based character education program. Priscilla, an accomplished musician and graduate of Juilliard, is also an active proponent of community and cultural programs, serving as a board member or supporter of Opera Theatre, Webster University Community Music School, Care and Counseling, Missouri Historical Society, St. Louis Arts and Education Council Wednesday Club, Bach Society, Variety Club and the St. Louis Symphony Society.

An American

Judge Theodore McMillian

Hero

T The grandson of slaves, Theodore McMillian was the first African American judge appointed in Missouri and the first named to the Eighth U.S. Circuit Court of Appeals. He is considered by many an American hero.

Born and reared in St. Louis, the eldest of 10 children, Judge McMillian worked as a train porter to support himself during high school and as a janitor to pay for college. After graduating from Lincoln College and Saint Louis University School of Law, where he ranked first in his class, he was appointed assistant city prosecutor and, in 1956, became the first African American named to a Missouri judgeship.

He then served as board chair of the Human Development Corporation in President Lyndon Johnson's War on Poverty program. And, in 1978, President Jimmy Carter appointed him to the Eighth U.S. Circuit Court of Appeals.

Judge McMillian continues to adjudicate in the Court of Appeals and is active with civic and charitable organizations as well. His honors are numerous and include the American Bar Association's Spirit of Excellence Award as well as the Bar Association of Metropolitan St. Louis Founder's Award and Distinguished Lawyer Award. He is also an Honorary Diplomat of the American Board of Trial Advocates.

And, Judge McMillian is a firm believer in the value of maturity: "We simply cannot lose or ignore the wisdom and experience of older people. They have so much to give."

"Often wisdom comes with age and that is such a valuable asset."

Judge Theodore McMillian, Missouri's first African American judge, has served as president of the National Council of Juvenile Court Judges, the Urban League of Metropolitan St. Louis, and the Herbert Hoover Boys and Girls Club, and on the executive committee of the St. Louis Crime Commission. He established the McMillian Scholarship for Minority Students at Saint Louis University, is a member of Phi Beta Kappa, an inductee of the National Bar Association Hall of Fame, and the recipient of honorary doctorates from Lincoln University, the University of Missouri-St. Louis, Saint Louis University and Harris-Stowe State College.

A Generous

Wilma Messing

Friend

When she was a little younger, Wilma Messing gave her volunteer service in person. Now, she prefers to support good causes financially. In both, over the years, she has been a generous friend of education and St. Louisans in need.

Born and reared in St. Louis, Mrs. Messing has long been exposed to and involved in charitable causes. Her parents emphasized a charitable attitude.

"I was raised to take care of people who needed help," she said. "When I was a child we didn't have much money, but I remember we used to have a tailor and a presser and my parents would invite them for dinner because we knew they didn't have enough money to always get a good home-cooked meal."

Her late husband, civic and business leader Roswell Messing, shared her philanthropic philosophy. The Wilma and Roswell Messing Faculty Award is given each year to a Webster University faculty member presenting the most promising curriculum-strengthening research project. The Messing Family Charitable Foundation supports minority scholarships at Southern Illinois University. And, Mrs. Messing continues today as a benefactor to Washington University, St. Louis University, and the University of Missouri. Her latest efforts are for the Crisis Nursery at Forest Park Hospital.

"I was able to give them a room and furnish it so it can be used for mothers and babies facing crisis situations," Mrs. Messing said. "I have been very fortunate in my life and feel privileged to be able to share with and give back to others."

"I have been very fortunate and feel privileged to share and give back.

Wilma Messing, a long-time friend to higher education as well as those with special needs, has received many honors and appointments for her efforts. They include: the *St. Louis Globe-Democrat* Woman of Achievement award; serving as a board member of Associates of St. Louis University Libraries and Washington University School of Art; being named Director Emeritus of Good Shepherd School, and Dance St. Louis. She has also served on the board of the National Council of Jewish Women and as the organization's local president.

"I don't believe in falling into a shell. For some people, gardening or playing golf makes them happy, and that is fine. But, it wouldn't do for me."

Building Structures
and Lives

I.E. Millstone

H is friends to describe him as a "softie with too much moxie to be a patsy," and "a civic conscience in shirtsleeves who gives without worrying, listens like a public relations counselor and works like a human bulldozer on one of his building projects."

I. E. Millstone, 96, is one of St. Louis' most prolific architectural engineers and philanthropists. His companies, Millstone Construction, Inc. and Millstone Bangert Construction, built Busch Stadium, the Federal Building, Mercantile Tower, and most of the city's public housing, roads and bridges. His own personal philanthropy supports dozens of annual scholarships in the fields of architecture, the arts and sciences, engineering and social work. Millstone's further commitments include lifetime memberships on the National Welfare Board and the United Hebrew Temple Board of Trustees, and serving as honorary lifetime chair of the Jewish Federation of St. Louis.

Although he has retired, he is in his Clayton office most days of the year, providing valuable advice to those running the companies now and overseeing his philanthropic efforts.

Millstone has always been and continues to be so involved, "Because I feel fortunate to have had such great opportunities," he said. "There is something inside me that says: 'You have to use your talents, your time and your money to be helpful to others.'"

I. E. Millstone is one of St. Louis' most productive builders and generous philanthropists. His honors and awards include: the William Greenleaf Eliot Society Award, the Saint Louis University Corporate Leadership Award, the Brotherhood Award from the National Conference of Christians and Jews, the Meritorious Achievement Award from the Urban League, the Torch of Liberty Award from B'nai B'rith, and the *Globe-Democrat* Humanitarian Award.

Conserving the Law,

James Moloney

the Land, the People

Three things define life for Jim Moloney. He is an attorney by trade, a charitable contributor to causes he believes in, and a life-long conservationist who loves the land. At 80 years of age, he is a very busy individual.

"I believe we should remain active," Moloney said. "It's the way to keep up both the body and the brain."

Every morning by the time he arrives at his office in Clayton, Moloney has read two newspapers, attended 8 a.m. Mass and driven 30 miles to work from his home in Pevely, listening to motivational and opera tapes all the way. An estate planner, probate and tax attorney, he spends a full day with corporate and individual clients, and still has time for civic and charitable activities including, his parish, St. Joseph's Catholic Church, Clayton Rotary, Fair St. Louis, United Way, White House Retreats, BirthRight, and Sierra Club.

However, in spite of the energetic atmosphere in which he seems to thrive, Moloney insists, "My heart and soul are on the porch of my log cabin overlooking the Current River."

Working in tandem with the Missouri Forestry Division, Moloney, the conservationist, has planted more than 200,000 pine and 20,000 black walnut trees on his Current River property. "I have always loved the land and feel we have an obligation to preserve and protect it," he said.

The perpetually active Moloney is also an advocate of river conservation. When he recalled that his grandfather swam across the Mississippi at the age of 80, Moloney vowed to do the same. In September 2003, with the backing of friends and family, he challenged and conquered the mighty river with determination and a strong swimming stroke.

"Some people say because they're older, they're no longer going to be involved, they're no longer going to work. That's a shame and a loss."

An attorney specializing in estate planning, probate and tax law, James Moloney is a graduate of Washington University with degrees in business and law. He is also an appointee, by Pope John Paul II, to the Equestrian Order of the Holy Sepulcher in recognition of his involvement in charitable causes, including World Missions and OBL Victory Mission. A conservationist as well, Moloney has planted thousands of trees along the Current River.

Home is Where

Marie Moore

the Heart Is

Marie Moore has a special place in her heart for a familiar red-headed clown, families of sick children, and a big old home in south St. Louis. She is a volunteer at the Ronald McDonald House on Park Avenue. Mrs. Moore spends much of her free time helping at the "home away from home" for families of children being treated at St. Louis hospitals.

She is a multi-task volunteer, doing whatever needs to be done to help with daily household operations and to assist the families that stay there. "I'm just happy to do something that helps families in crisis situations," she said.

Mrs. Moore, 77, is well known for regularly bringing in bakery treats, taking work home or putting in extra hours during the weeks before special events. She willingly volunteers extra days or covers for other volunteers who may be ill or on vacation.

But for the most part, she is simply a "people person" whose heart is with the families who stay at the Ronald McDonald House while their children are hospitalized. What she does to ease their anxiety and to make them feel at home, "does as much for me as it does for them," Mrs. Moore said. "There are so many intangible rewards and so many wonderful people."

"Being a volunteer – there are so many rewards and still so much to be done."

Marie Moore is very much a "people person" who volunteers her time and her heart at one of the two local Ronald McDonald Houses. She helps to provide a welcoming, comfortable and affordable place for the families of sick, hospitalized children to temporarily call home.

"The worst thing you can do is nothing. Be useful, because anything you don't use withers away."

Practicing for a

Homer Nash, MD

Better Today

Being 77, Dr. Homer Nash can look back three-quarters of a century, and although he concedes contemporary society is far from perfect, he has little love for what some call the "good old days."

"You may think things are bad today," Dr. Nash said. "But it's a lot better than it used to be. In 1900, the lifespan was 45 to 49 years. Tuberculosis was rampant and there was no effective treatment for syphilis and gonorrhea. There was a lot of child labor. Women had no rights."

As a pediatrician, he has seen great strides in medicine. As a southerner, he has seen the lessening of prejudice among races and cultures. As a church member, a vestryman at All Saints Episcopal Church, he has seen a growing community involvement on the part of religious groups.

"It's not productive to dwell on the past," Dr. Nash said. "You can only try to make each day better than the last one." That philosophy is what propelled him into medicine. Today, Dr. Nash maintains a full pediatric practice with the help of one of his five daughters, Dr. Alison Nash, who joined him in 1989. Together, they care for infants, children and teens both physically and emotionally. And, even after all these years, his work remains exceedingly gratifying for Dr. Nash.

"I just love the kids," he said. "They provide the opportunity for me to help someone every day and to help make today better than yesterday."

Dr. Homer Nash comes from a medical family. His father and an older sister were physicians and his uncle was a dentist. Their influence and a desire to make the world a little better a day at a time propelled Dr. Nash into medicine. A graduate of Moorehouse College in Georgia and Meharry Medical College in Tennessee, he served his residency at the former Homer G. Phillips Hospital. He has been practicing pediatrics in St. Louis ever since.

To Education,

Kathryn Nelson

With Love

Kathryn Nelson is many things: college professor and teacher, administrator, missionary, social worker, family educator, and consultant. There are few St. Louis educational and cultural programs to which she has not given her time, her talents and herself.

Raised in the South during the height of racial prejudice and conflict, Mrs. Nelson realized that a child's view of the world is shaped early in life. That realization is the foundation of her philosophy that positive role models and good early education are essential to children's healthy and successful development.

Mrs. Nelson came to St. Louis in 1952, following a missionary effort in Haiti, and served as a social worker at the Annie Malone Children's Home. Later, she taught in the St. Louis Public Schools and became the first director of the Junior League's Junior Kindergarten program. It became a model for those training to teach in the then-new Head Start program in the St. Louis area.

At St. Louis Community College, she directed one of 13 national projects charged with developing credentialing and training for Head Start workers. She helped, as a member of Confluence St. Louis, to create the report, "Valuing Our Diversity: A New Vision for St. Louis," and served as co-chair of the implementation committee.

With expertise and great love, Mrs. Nelson continues to write, organize workshops and consult with groups on major educational, family and youth issues.

"I am a firm believer in life-long learning," she said. "It allows us to grow and to develop an understanding of what has gone before, what is happening now, and what to strive for in the future."

"As seniors, we can continue to learn, to contribute and to grow."

Kathryn Nelson is a recipient of the 2003 Leadership Award from FOCUS St. Louis "for her 50 years of extraordinary dedication and service to the people of metropolitan St. Louis." The prestigious award recognizes her for creating quality educational opportunities, demonstrating innovative solutions, fostering regional cooperation, improving racial equality and social justice, and promoting stronger communities. Mrs. Nelson holds a Master's Degree in Christian Education as well as an honorary Doctorate of Humanities from Saint Louis University.

"The knowledge and experience that come with age, is like good wine."

Designing

Gyo Obata

Dreams

A distinguished architect, Gyo Obata has contributed much to the architectural beauty of America. It is a land he loves even though as a Japanese American teenager living in California during World War II, he narrowly escaped being sent to an internment camp with his artist parents. His acceptance at Washington University brought him to the Midwest where there was far less prejudice and no forced confinement of Japanese Americans.

Sixty years later, with degrees in architecture and numerous awards, Obata chairs and is the head of design for Hellmuth, Obata and Kassabaum, one of the country's largest architectural, engineering and planning firms. Among his projects are St. Louis' Metropolitan Square, Missouri History Museum Emerson Center, the National Air and Space Museum in the Smithsonian Institution, the new Pavilion at the Japanese American Museum, Levi's Plaza at Levi Strauss headquarters in San Francisco, Exxon Corporate headquarters in Irving, Texas, Foley Square in New York, and King Khalid International Airport in Saudi Arabia.

Architecture, he says, precludes retirement of the mind. "In order to design something I have to really understand my client's vision and needs. There is a lot of thinking and research involved, and I think that is a way of getting your mind to continue to work."

Seniors in all walks of life have much to contribute, Obata indicated. "With all the knowledge and experience that comes with age, it's like good wine, to be shared and enjoyed."

Gyo Obata, a revered architect for six decades, continues to craft outstanding architecture with a design philosophy of creating functional space that also enhances life.

Gotta

Opal Otis

Dance

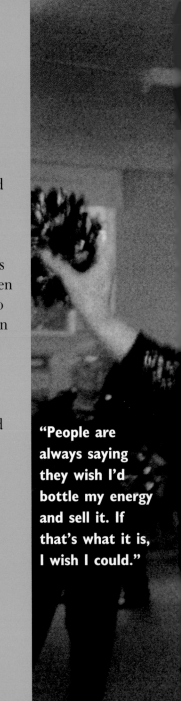

Opal Otis has danced through life and at 91 is still kicking up her heels. For 65 years, she has taught children, teen-agers and seniors to enjoy dance as much as she does. And, she has no plans any time soon to put her feet up on a comfortable cushion rather than down on a varnished floor.

For Mrs. Otis, "dance fever" hit when she was a little girl. She took lessons at a community center and from then on performed, taught and enjoyed. When she and her late husband, Warren, married in 1938, she passed the fever on to him. With a repertoire of ballroom, foxtrot, swing, disco, waltz and all the Latin dances, the couple taught classes at the Kirkwood YMCA and numerous other locations for 40 years. They even went international, taking their pupils on 35 cruises all over the world and entertaining aboard ship.

As a YMCA volunteer, Mrs. Otis organized the "Tailgate Bouncers" for junior and senior high teens. For more than 18 years, young dancers practiced weekly and entertained at hospitals, nursing homes, retirement centers, detention facilities, conventions and fairs.

Today, Mrs. Otis concentrates on bringing dance and dance / exercise to other seniors. She teaches five classes a week at her church, a senior center, and a retirement community. "You've got to make yourself move," she said, "whether you like it or not. That's the secret of staying young – just to get up and do something."

"People are always saying they wish I'd bottle my energy and sell it. If that's what it is, I wish I could."

1

Opal Otis has "gotta" dance. At 91, she still cuts a fine step across the dance floor. And, after 65 years of teaching others to do the same, the sound of her pupils' dancing feet echoes across the entire St. Louis area.

A Heart for

Robert Paine, MD

Health Care

H is medical specialty is Cardiology. His life specialty is also a matter of the heart. Dr. Robert Paine has one large enough for hundreds of patients who otherwise wouldn't have ready access to a physician.

Dr. Paine, who is retired from daily medical practice, heads a free health screening clinic – the University City East Health Protection and Education Service – which serves people who are health care deprived. Many are Chinese immigrants; some are young people, including children brought by their parents; others are simply people with little money for health care and no insurance.

One Saturday morning each month, Dr. Paine and about 20 physicians, medical students and nurses, all of whom he has recruited and volunteer their time, set up shop in the University City Library auditorium. They staff screening stations where people can get counsel on and tests for anemia, depression, cancer, diabetes, hearing problems; heart, lung, kidney and digestive diseases; high blood pressure, high cholesterol, STD, HIV and AIDS.

Each person receives a copy of "My Medical Handbook." It includes space for medical records and personal health information, a section on communicating with health professionals and understanding symptoms, as well as a community directory detailing where other services and assistance may be obtained.

"If you walk into one of our sessions, you get a feeling of 'gosh, this is wonderful,'" Dr. Paine said. "These people never had a chance to have a doctor, never had the opportunity to sit down and talk with a doctor and here they all are – 70 to 80 at each session – finally getting the help they need. It's very gratifying, very special."

"Mankind has tremendous potential. That potential doesn't run out when you hit age 65."

Dr. Robert Paine, the son and grandson of doctors, is Emeritus Professor of Clinical Medicine for the Washington University School of Medicine. He is a graduate of Harvard University Medical School and came to St. Louis to intern at Barnes-Jewish Hospital. Considered among the finest clinicians, he served as Chief of Medicine at St. Luke's Hospital and practiced cardiology there as well as at Barnes.

"So I've passed the test. I'm retired more than 10 years now and I'm still alive."

Sharing

Tzy Cheng Peng, Ph.D.

America

D r. Tzy Chen Peng, a naturalized American of Chinese ancestry, is in many ways an ambassador and a mentor to Chinese Americans and immigrants in the St. Louis area. An American citizen since 1962, Dr. Peng was an immigrant himself when he came to the USA in the early 1950s to attend college. Now, he taps his more than 50 years of experience as an American to mentor, inform, and advise Chinese people new to the St. Louis area.

Often, in the local Chinese community, where there are numerous people of the same ancestry congregated together, "they don't learn about the bigger society, because they don't have to," Dr Peng said. "They can speak Chinese only and get by; they can carry on traditional Chinese ways. But we live in America and it's important to be American, too."

In order to assist with that process, Dr. Peng, 72, monitors current events and legislation and holds town hall meetings to inform Chinese residents of what it all means and the effect on them. During election years, he conducts classes on politics and the voting process and assists those who are eligible to register to vote. He is a volunteer language instructor, teaching English as a second language for new arrivals. And, as president of Chinese American Forum, Inc., he is instrumental in the publication of a not-for-profit, informational Chinese American magazine that circulates in the metropolitan area.

All of this is his mission, he says, because he wants to share his adopted country with others. "The United States, although it has its faults, is basically good. It is a good system; I especially respect the wisdom of our founding fathers."

Dr. Tzy Chen Peng, a mentor to St. Louis-area Chinese Americans, has served as president of the St. Louis Chinese Society and the St. Louis chapter of the Organization of Chinese Americans. A graduate of Northwestern University, and holding a Master's Degree and a Doctorate in mechanical engineering, Dr. Peng was, before his retirement, an associate senior scientist at McDonnell Douglas Research Laboratories in St. Louis, an associate scientist at General Motors Defense Research Laboratory, and a research scientist in the Aerospace Division of Boeing.

"Not doing any-
thing is to die of
boredom."

Passing on

James Primm, Ph.D.

St. Louis' History

James Neal Primm's passion as an educator, historian and author is evident in the work he has done to bring St. Louis history to life. Eighty-five years young, Dr. Primm, an expert on the city's past, is Curators' Professor Emeritus at the University of Missouri-St. Louis and teaching a history course for graduate students.

His love for teaching and sharing history began early on. While working on a Bachelor's Degree from Northeast Missouri State in the late 1930s, he taught children in one-room schoolhouses. He came to St. Louis in 1965 to join the academic team that helped to found UMSL.

He has authored several books – most written after his "retirement" – that bring St. Louis history not only to life, but into focus. His book, *Lion of the Valley, St. Louis, 1764-1980*, is in its fourth edition. He has also published *A Foregone Conclusion, the Founding of the St. Louis Federal Reserve Bank*; *Germans for a Free Missouri*, with Steven Rowan; *The Economy of 19th Century St. Louis*; and is a contributing author to *St. Louis in the Century of Henry Shaw: Beyond the Garden Wall*.

Dr. Primm has received many honors for his writing, including UMSL's Thomas Jefferson Award. The Missouri History Museum sponsors an annual James Neal Primm Lecture in History in his honor.

"What you want to do is enjoy life," he said in reflecting on the prospect of continuing one's profession well beyond the standard retirement time. "As a senior, I need something to do simply to feel better."

Dr. James Neal Primm holds a Master's Degree in history and a Doctorate from the University of Missouri-Columbia where he served as an instructor and associate professor of history before moving to Hiram College in Ohio where he was, in turn, dean, vice president and president. A veteran of World War II, he served at Guadalcanal, Tarawa and Kwajalein, and left the Navy in 1946 as a lieutenant commander.

"You don't want to rust out; you want to wear out. God granted us the ability to wear out."

Rust Not —

Harold & Virginia Schreimann

Wear Out

Harold and Virginia Schreimann – known to their friends as Hank and Gini – long ago agreed that "it's better to wear out than to rust out." The facts that Hank retired from an active business career and that Gini has undergone two knee replacements have not slowed them down. Their volunteer lists are voluminous and their participation is ongoing.

Hank is a delegate to the White House Conference on Education, a Scottish Rite Mason and Shriner, and serves on the Advisory Committee of St. Louis Community College. He chairs the Reciprocal Relations Committee of the University Club, and is president of the Eliot Society at Washington University. He is president of the Carlyle Townhomes Association. And, at his church, Ladue Chapel Presbyterian, he is an elder and a deacon and chairs the Executive Committee as well as St. Andrew's Memorial Garden.

Gini serves on the Advisory Board of Care & Counseling. She is an elder and an officer of the Women's Association at Ladue Chapel; serves as secretary of her PEO chapter; and is chair of several committees including the Wednesday Club, an educational and philanthropic organization. She is also a great supporter of the St. Louis Symphony Orchestra Volunteer Association as a long-time board member and chair of several committees.

"The most important thing is not to be thinking about yourself all the time," Gini said. "You just need to get up and 'do.' And, if you can't, just call a friend and offer a kind word."

"I would rather be a participant than a spectator," said Hank. "I'd rather go out and help others than sit at home and watch television."

Hank and Gini Schreimann, both born and raised in Normandy, are long-time supporters of and participants in community causes. Hank, a graduate of Washington University, is a professional engineer and past president of his own company, MSI Ltd.

Gini, a graduate of the University of Wisconsin, worked at Meremac College for a number of years in counseling services before turning her attention to volunteer and civic efforts.

Living

Floyd Smith

History

With more than a century of life to his credit, Floyd Smith is a living history book. He has seen and experienced phenomenal changes, celebrated a multitude of both personal and global triumphs and mourned many tragedies. He has watched tyrants and heroes come and go. He has known peace and war. As a child, he sometimes rode a mule to a one-room schoolhouse; as a man, he has seen astronauts ride rockets to the moon. He survived prejudice and segregation and embraced civil rights. Floyd Smith *lived* the Twentieth Century. It has been, he says, like watching the birth of "a whole new world."

Born in 1900 in Sweet Home, Arkansas, Smith came to St. Louis with his mother in 1904. He is sure of the date because, "the World's Fair was going on and I remember seeing it. The streets weren't paved; there were wooden sidewalks, but it was a big, busy city and that right there was the start of a whole new world for me.

"Like a lot of other children," he added, "I went to school just half a day and then worked in the afternoon in the fields." Smith has always worked – hard. Primarily, he was in the hauling business, transporting sand and gravel for construction, and wood and coal to fuel-hungry customers. "Never been afraid of work," he said.

Although now confined to a wheelchair, Smith remains active. He lives independently at Gillespie Village senior apartments with the help of a part-time aide. His church, Cote Brilliante Presbyterian, and his faith are all-important. "I am an old-fashioned, religious Christian man," he said.

Floyd Smith attributes his long life to, "doing what God wants me to do and that is treating everybody as my brother and my sister."

Words of wisdom for the Twenty-first Century.

"What can we do that's important when we get old? Help other people. To me, that seems like the most important thing."

At 103, Floyd Smith still gives of himself and his talents to others. An "old-fashioned, religious Christian man," he daily offers up prayers for friends. His more worldly contributions consist of wonderful food and baked items. An expert cook, he regularly invites friends in for dinner, and bakes cakes for everyone from his doctor to elderly neighbors and residents of the Home for the Blind.

Eternal Optimist

Verna Smith, Ph.D.

and Volunteer

For Verna Green Smith, retirement is nearly as busy as the many years she spent as a high school teacher and journalist. Even though she is strictly a volunteer, she has never stopped working and never stopped learning.

Several mornings each week, Mrs. Smith volunteers her time and talents at OASIS, writing, editing and proofreading the senior enrichment organization's materials and publications. She is also on the OASIS speaker's bureau, specializing in oral histories and peer counseling.

"It is so important to keep learning, to keep on improving the mind," she says.

From her creative mind come stories that, as a volunteer storyteller, she shares with schoolchildren and retirement home residents. Mrs. Smith, in her 80s, could, in fact, be the subject of her own stories. Always anxious to try new things, she was one of those people chosen to carry the Olympic Torch on its cross-country journey to the 1996 games in Atlanta.

As a journalist, Mrs. Smith has been a member of the Press Club of Metropolitan St. Louis for 16 years, serving as first vice president and treasurer, and on the club's finance and Media Person of the Year committees. She is active in the National Federation of Press Women, Missouri Affiliate, and coordinates media archives activity at the Public Library.

Forest Park Forever has the benefit of her participation as do the Older Women's League and the Mathews-Dickey Boys Club, where she has lectured on journalism careers. At Stephan Memorial United Methodist Church, she narrates Christmas and Easter cantatas.

"Older Americans have so much talent, experience and know-how to share," she says. "I am the eternal optimist. I believe we can do it all and do it well."

"I believe, as seniors, we have to keep going and keep giving,"

With a Bachelor's Degree in journalism, a Master's Degree and a Ph.D. in education, Verna Green Smith was well-equipped to teach. With an abundance of energy and a caring attitude, she is a very well-equipped volunteer. Her many hours of service to community organizations have been followed by awards and honors. They include: the OWL Women of Worth Award, the Missouri Press Women Quest Award, and inclusion in *Who's Who of American Women, National Register of Prominent Americans and International Notables, Community Leaders and Noteworthy Americans, Who's Who in the Midwest,* and *Personalities of the West and Midwest.*

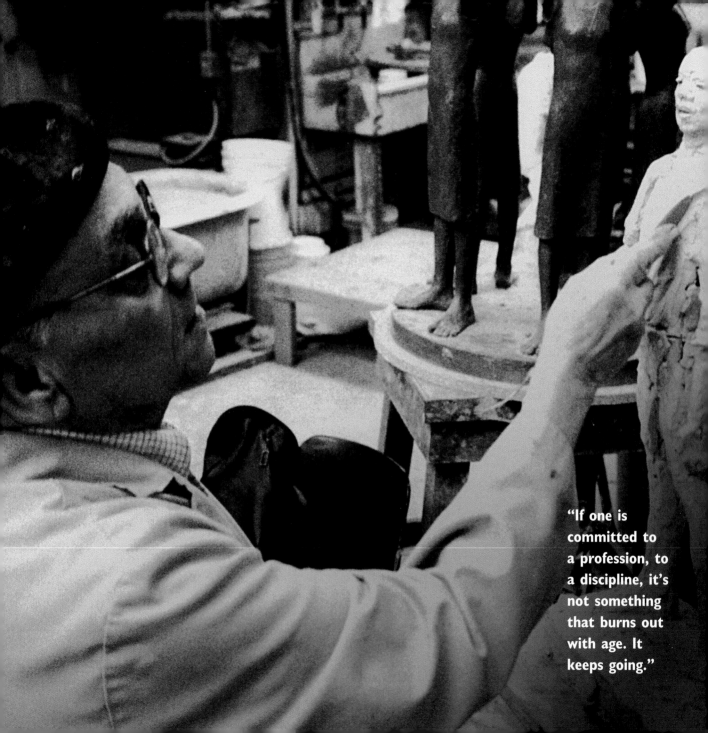

"If one is committed to a profession, to a discipline, it's not something that burns out with age. It keeps going."

For Art's

Rudy Torrini

Sake

When a woman in her 70s – a would-be artist – asked Rudy Torrini whether he thought she was too old to take up drawing, he told her: "Absolutely not; ideas and creativity have nothing to do with age."

Age has only enhanced the art of Rudy Torrini. He is one of the most prolific and distinguished sculptors in the nation, with his work on display in many churches, parks, museums and other venues. For Torrini, it is a total commitment.

"Everything I do is directed to my vocation and that's the way I choose for it to be," he said. "It's very, very satisfying and gratifying."

His studio, a building next to his South County home, is filled with his work – some completed, some in progress. One sculpture on which he is now working is that of Crispus Attucks, a former slave, the first American soldier and the first African American to die in the American Revolution.

Torrini's inspiration comes from a number of sources, not the least of which is his own passionate creativity. Commissioned work is the product of his talent and imagination and the requirements of the individual or organization doing the commissioning. An example is a figure of Jesus as a little boy that Torrini was commissioned to do by an Omaha, Nebraska church for a children's courtyard playground. Since how the young Jesus looked is a mystery, Torrini had to create his appearance while still meeting the expectations of church leaders. It is a creative challenge on which Torrini thrives.

"I'm fortunate in my vocation in that I'm never bored," he said. "One work triggers enthusiasm for another and I never tire of doing what I do."

The art of sculptor Rudy Torrini is well known in St. Louis and around the nation. His work includes sculptures of Italian immigrants in front of St. Andrew's Church on The Hill; the St. Louis Police Memorial in front of the Civil Courts Building downtown; a tribute to soccer players at St. Louis Soccer Park; the statue of Pope John Paul II across Lindell from Saint Louis University; a statue of Dr. Martin Luther King Jr. in Fountain Park; and a memorial in Ruma, Illinois to the five Catholic nuns who were murdered while serving in Africa.

A Creator of

Blanche Touhill, Ph.D.

Opportunities

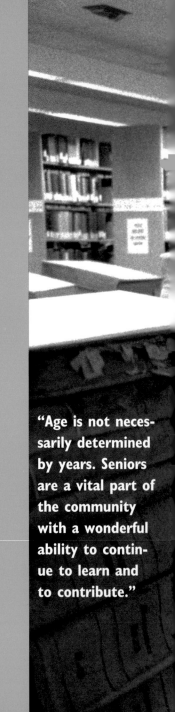

When Dr. Blanche Touhill retired in 2003 from her position as chancellor of the University of Missouri-St. Louis she told well-wishers: "For most of my adult life, I have wanted to be only two things: a teacher and the chancellor of UMSL. I have lived those dreams. And I thank God for my good fortune. But time moves on and so must I — making room for other dreamers and other doers."

Dr. Touhill, 71, has always been a dreamer and a doer. From the time she arrived at the UMSL campus in 1965 to teach history until and beyond her retirement, she has had a profound impact on local higher education. Dr. Touhill scored high marks as a popular instructor and respected researcher, as the first woman to chair the Faculty Senate and to serve as Vice Chancellor for Academic Affairs. But she is primarily known as the school's forward-thinking chancellor who successfully enhanced and expanded UMSL as the "university of opportunity" for the community.

"Underpinning all the things I've done throughout my career is a belief in providing public education to the people of the St. Louis area," Dr. Touhill said. "Without affordable public education, many of our citizens cannot break out of the situations in which they find themselves."

Appropriately, Dr. Touhill is writing a history of UMSL – looking back in order to help those who follow her continue moving forward.

"Age is not necessarily determined by years. Seniors are a vital part of the community with a wonderful ability to continue to learn and to contribute."

Dr. Blanche Touhill is forever a part of the University of Missouri-St. Louis. During 37 years there – 12 as chancellor – she led thousands of students, and faculty. Her efforts have produced many awards, including being named the 1997 Citizen of the Year by the *St. Louis Post-Dispatch.* "Off-campus" she is a civic leader, serving on boards and committees of the Metropolitan St. Louis Arts and Education Council, Catholic Youth Services, Girl Scouts of St. Louis President's Advisory Council, St. Louis' Art Museum, Science Center, Sheldon Concert Hall, and the BJC Committee on Life-Long Learning.

'S' for

Marvin S. Wool

Success

Marvin S. Wool is not one to countenance failure. His middle initial may very well stand for "success."

At 74, he is president and CEO of Dash Multi-Corp., a holding company with 11 subsidiaries that include manufacturing plants in Missouri, Georgia, Mississippi, New Jersey, California and North Carolina. They produce plastic raw materials, coated fabrics, flooring products and sales in excess of $138 million. It all grew from one small plastics company that Wool founded in 1973.

Then there is Allegiant Bancorp. Wool is board chair and CEO of the bank holding company with 15 locations in the St. Louis area and eastern Missouri.

But Dash and Allegiant were not his first successful ventures. In 1964, Wool started his own chemical company that was sold six years later to a company listed on the New York Stock Exchange.

Today, observers credit an entrepreneurial spirit and strong leadership for Wool's success. He concedes those are important factors, but points out that as both he and his ventures mature, he continues to be involved and to reinvest in both the companies, their employees and communities.

"I believe that regardless of age, we should keep on taking part, keep on reinvesting," Wool said, "not just our dollars, but also ourselves."

That, he indicated, is the formula for success.

> **"As you grow older, the more you stay active — both body and brain — the more satisfying your life will be."**

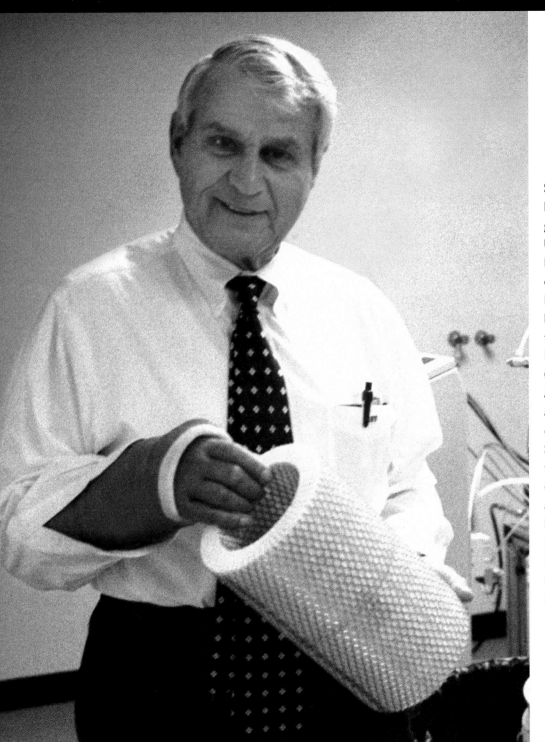

St. Louis businessman Marvin Wool is a graduate of Saint Louis University with a Bachelor's Degree in chemistry and a Master's Degree in business administration. He serves on the Board of the Jewish Community Centers Association, is immediate past president and current chair of the St. Louis Chapter of the American Society of Technion, and an active member of the Saint Louis University DuBourg Society, the Missouri Botanical Garden and the St. Louis Zoo.

"Being seniors we can use all the experience and knowledge we've gained and put it to work right now."

Together a

James and Myrtice Young

Volunteer 'Force'

"Togetherness" is the key word in the lives of James and Myrtice Young. In their 70s and married 49 years, they have created for themselves a volunteer effort they share with dedication and enthusiasm.

Both are educators – James spent 26 years with the University City schools as a teacher, director of alternative schools and high school business manager, and Myrtice has a degree in elementary and early childhood education. Retirement came in 1995, but not separation from the school system.

They are volunteer tutors for the system's students, assist with field trips, and each spring turn teacher gardeners at several elementary schools. "We help the kids plant and care for gardens with lettuce, carrots, spinach and such," James said. "When everything is ready, we gather it all in and make salads for every child in school. It's great."

They also volunteer in community service. They are caretakers of community flower beds for U. City in Bloom and are co-chairs of the University City AARP membership committee. "Then, one day a week we volunteer at the Lupus Foundation," Myrtice said. "And once a month I go to the Kingdom House where I serve on the board," She is also on the board of Kids' Place, an after-school tutoring program at a local church. Attend a Fox Theatre performance on a Sunday night and you'll see the Youngs at the door greeting theatergoers and taking tickets.

Why spend perhaps more hours volunteering than they did working?

"Life has been good to us," James said, "and we want to give back. We haven't accumulated any wealth but we have health and kids. When I think of the kind of contributions that we as seniors can make, it's all very worthwhile."

James and Myrtice Young are in agreement that as a couple they have much to contribute as volunteers. Together, they provide tutoring and attention to children, help to beautify the neighborhood, work on behalf of seniors and those who are ill, and contribute to the arts. Their volunteer "togetherness" benefits both the Youngs and the community.

Our
St. Andrew's Resources for Seniors
History

I t is an exciting and crucial time to be involved with providing and maintaining services for older adults. They are one of the fastest growing and most dynamic segments of the population. They are our grandparents; they are our parents, our neighbors and friends. They are us.

St. Andrew's Resources for Seniors (STARS) began serving older people more than 42 years ago – before it was the fashionable and politically correct thing to do. Consequently, STARS is one of the most knowledgeable sponsors and providers of senior-related housing and supportive services. Like the older adults we serve, we have expertise born of experience, goals born of recognizing a need, and heart born of relating to others.

It comes from a Mission: *In our faith-based tradition, we will nurture the spirit of the older adult and community through the creation and support of choices and options.* With that commission, STARS was born in 1961 as the Episcopal Presbyterian Foundation for the Aging, a joint endeavor of the Episcopal Diocese of Missouri and the Presbytery of Giddings-Lovejoy, Presbyterian Church (USA).

Today, St. Andrew's is a leader among senior services advocates by providing beneficial services, by meeting needs, and by truly caring about older adults and their families. STARS' services comprise sponsorship and management of retirement communities, assisted living communities, nursing care centers, subsidized housing for seniors with limited financial resources, and innovative in-home care and community services.

Included are:
- Housing for low-income seniors through partnerships with churches and other not-for-profit groups, financed by U.S. Housing and Urban Development: Almira Manor, Friendly Village Apartments, Gillespie Village, Mercy Seat Apartments, St. Andrew's of Jennings, and Zion Corner Apartments. There are three more in development today.
- Tower Grove Manor retirement apartments on South Grand Avenue.
- Brooking Park assisted living and skilled nursing community in Chesterfield.
- The Willows retirement apartments in Chesterfield.
- St. Andrew's Management Services, providing management and consulting services to organizations, groups and individuals interested in supplying housing and health services to the elderly.
- St. Andrew's At-Home Services, providing care and services to older adults with the goal of helping them maintain their independence and remain in their own homes, and providing support and care for the family caregiver.
- St. Andrew's Spiritual Outreach Ministry, touching the lives of homebound and senior community residents through visits, a quarterly newsletter, and by serving as a senior-focused resource for churches and clergy.

...daily we look to our Vision and ultimate goal: *A society where all older adults are respected, productive, secure and fulfilled.*

Throughout our many years of service to the community, St. Andrew's has remained true to its Mission; and now daily we look to our Vision and ultimate goal: *A society where all older adults are respected, productive, secure and fulfilled.*

St. Andrew's

Making So
Our Contributors
Much Possible

Special appreciation is afforded

Stifel, Nicolaus & Company

for their particularly

generous support of

Ageless – Remarkable St. Louisans

It is our contributors' generosity and support
that has transported *Ageless–Remarkable St. Louisans*
from possibility to reality.

GOLD LEVEL

Paric Corporation

SILVER LEVEL

BKD

CareLinc, LLC

Enterprise Rent-A-Car
  Foundation

Bill Freund

Interlock Pharmacy

Lawrence Group Architects, Inc.

Mary Alice and John Ryan

Saur & Associates

Shaughnessy Family Foundation

Southwest Bank

BRONZE LEVEL

Altman Charter

Ann Bannes

Civil & Environmental
  Consultants, Inc.

Alverne Fiddmont-Hood

McKesson Medical Surgical

Ken Marx

Fairfax Pollnow

John Pollock

Walter Knoll Florist

Werremeyer | Floresca

FRIENDS PREMIERE LEVEL

Bommarito Automotive Group

Chris Buckley

Dr. Thomas A. Dew

Mark Goran

Gershman Investment Corp.

Presbytery of Giddings-Lovejoy

J&J Siding & Window Sales, Inc.

Bob Lucy

Diane Meatheany

New Providence Presbyterian Church

Rt. Rev. Hays Rockwell

Bruce Russell

Sodexho Senior Services

FRIENDS LEVEL

Barbara Boeving

Edith Brady

Theresa Bradford

Christopher Brown

Ann Bussing

Dean Team of Ballwin

Sondra Denk

Joan Devine

Carol DiSanza

Rev. Canon Thomas Doyle

Gregory Elliott

Betty Ette

Mary Gordon

Ronald Gribbins

Michelle Grimm

H.B.D. Contracting, Inc.

Paul Hales

Jane Hamilton

Celia Hosler

Jeannette Huey

ISU Corp.

Natalie Jablonski

Sandra James

Miriam Jenkins

Marilyn Krisanic

Martha Kay Larsen

Charlotte Lehmann

Lowenbaum Partnership

Jefferson L. Miller

Harry Moppins, Jr.

Everett Page

Planells Family

Cheryl Proyaseng

Lynn Reyner

Rev. Joanne Robbins

William Schoenhard

Keith Shaw

Linda Shillito

Frank Siano

Sheryl Steele

Mark Templeton

Tyler Troutman

Ronald Unterreiner

Toni Vaughn

Douglas & Jeanne Wilton

Steve Woodruff

Bill Zukoski

In Honor of Eugene J. Koester

In Memory of Michael Sprehe